WONDER
STARTERS

Sleep

Pictures by JOHN MOUSEDALE

Published by WONDER BOOKS
A Division of Grosset & Dunlap, Inc.
A NATIONAL GENERAL COMPANY
51 Madison Avenue New York, N.Y. 10010

About Wonder Starters

Wonder Starters are vocabulary controlled information books for young children. More than ninety per cent of the words in the text will be in the reading vocabulary of the vast majority of young readers. Word and sentence length have also been carefully controlled.

Key new words associated with the topic of each book are repeated with picture explanations in the Starters dictionary at the end. The dictionary can also be used as an index for teaching children to look things up.

Teachers and experts have been consulted on the content and accuracy of the books.

Published in the United States by Wonder Books, a Division of Grosset & Dunlap, Inc., a National General Company.

ISBN: 0-448-09658-7 (Trade Edition)
ISBN: 0-448-06378-6 (Library Edition)

Printed and bound in the United States.

I am asleep.
The sheets and blankets keep me warm.
My pillow is soft.

A long time ago
people slept on dry grass.
Animal skins kept them warm.
They did not have pillows.

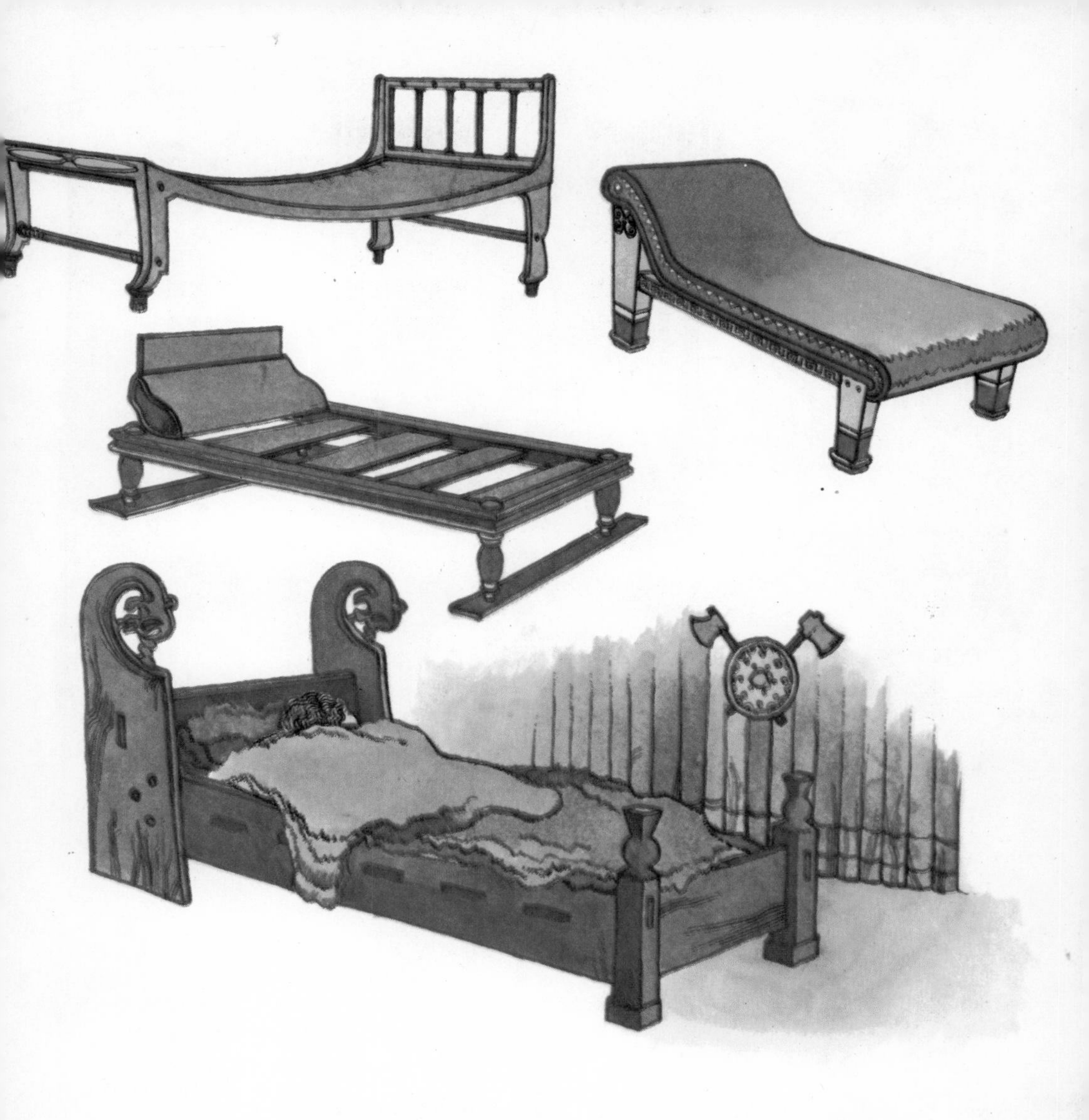

The ground can be hard and cold.
So people made beds.
The beds were softer.

Some people had very big beds.
They had four-poster beds.
You can see the four posts.
Curtains kept out cold air.

This was a king's bed.
People came to see the king in bed.
They helped him to get up.

Sailors used to sleep in hammocks.
Hammocks swing about.
Sailors could take them down
in the day.

You can sleep on trains.
These people are in a train.
They will sleep in berths.

People in Japan
sleep on the floor.
They roll the beds up
in the daytime.

Some campers sleep on the ground.
Some sleep on cots.
Soldiers sleep on cots, too.

Sometimes climbers sleep on ledges.
Ropes keep them from falling off.

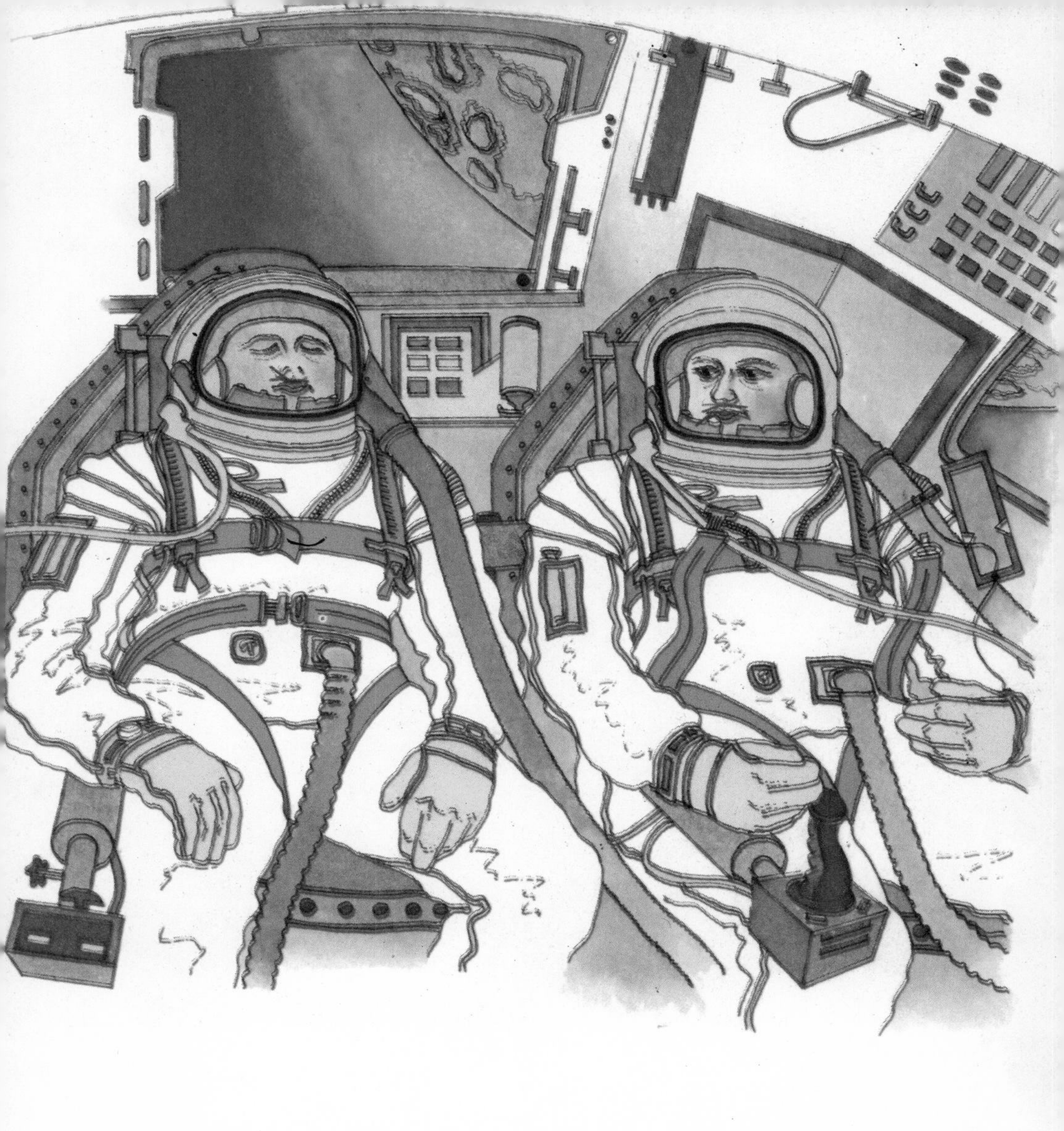

Astronauts sleep with straps around them.
Straps keep them from floating around.

Some people can sleep anywhere.
This is Napoleon.
He was a soldier who slept in the field.

Some babies sleep
on their mother's back.

Fakirs can sleep on nails.

Most animals lie down to sleep.
Many animals curl up
when they sleep.

Elephants can sleep standing up
or lying down.
Giraffes sleep standing up.

Bats sleep in the daytime.
Bats sleep upside down.
Mice sleep in the daytime.
Owls sleep in the daytime.

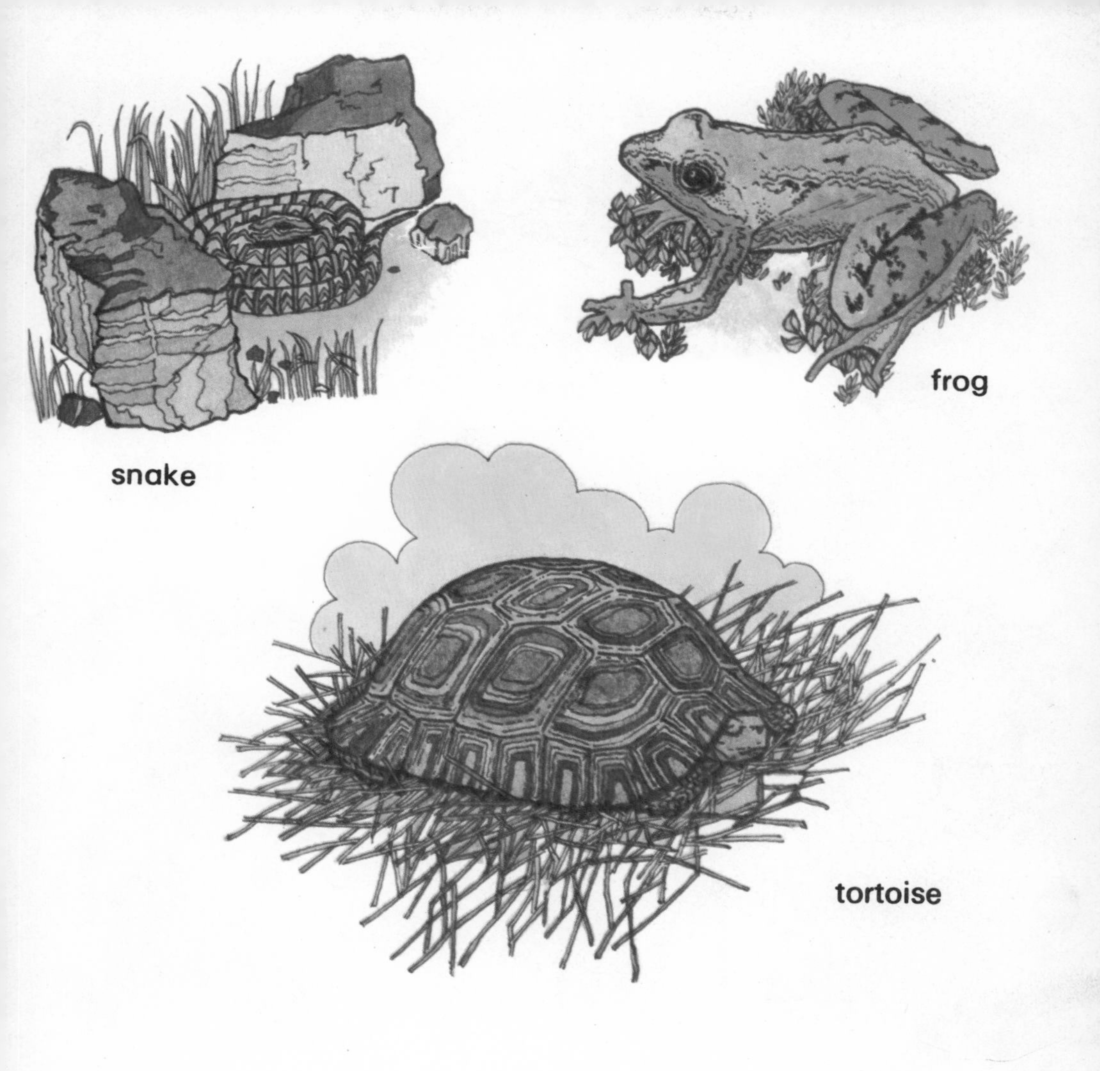

Some animals stay asleep
most of the winter.
They hibernate.

You move about in
your sleep.
You move many times.

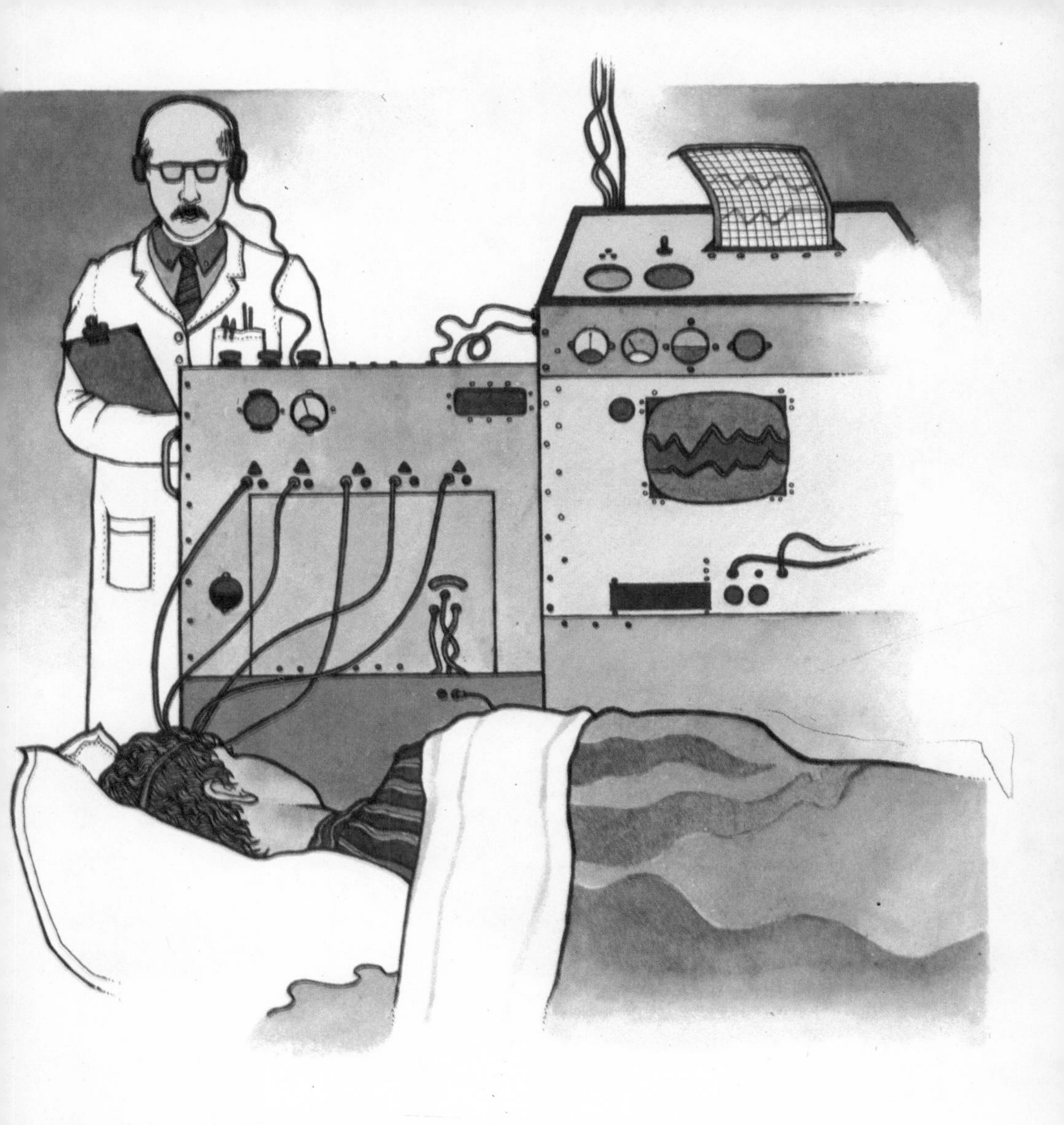

Scientists find out
what happens when you sleep.
They have studied sleep.

Some painters paint pictures of their dreams.

Long ago Caesar's wife
dreamed he would be killed.
He did not believe her,
but he was killed.

See for yourself

Try to remember
a dream.
See if you can paint
a picture of your dream.

Starter's **Sleep** words

sheet
(page 1)

blanket
(page 1)

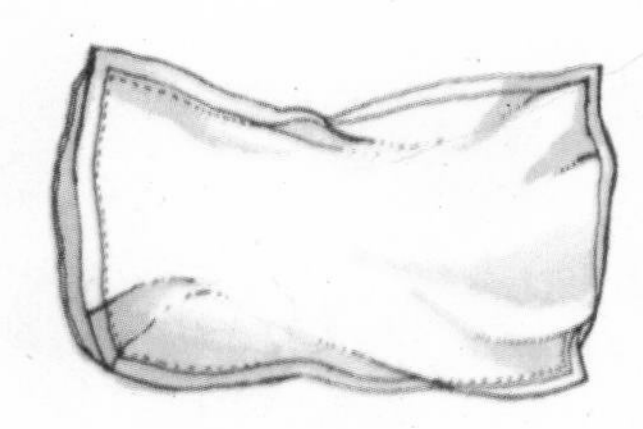

pillow
(page 1)

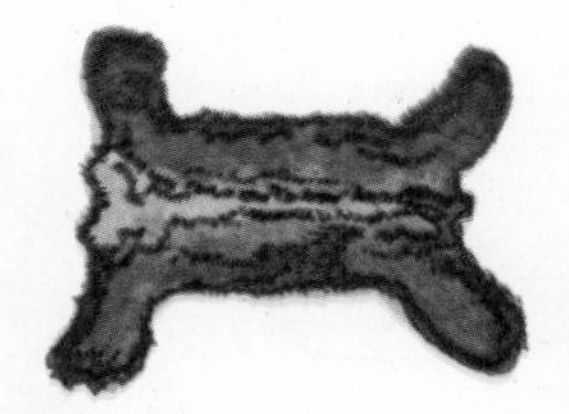

animal skin
(page 2)

four-poster bed
(page 4)

curtains
(page 4)

hammock
(page 6)

berth
(page 7)

cot
(page 9)

climber
(page 10)

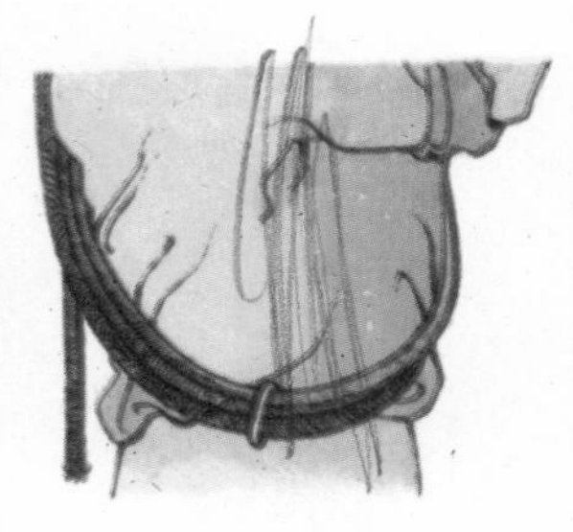

ropes
(page 10)

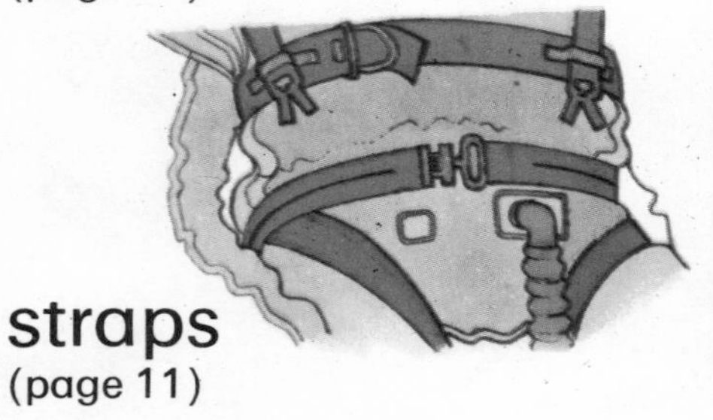

straps
(page 11)

soldier
(page 12)

bat
(page 16)

mice
(page 16)

owl
(page 16)